WEDDING
CUPCAKES

JOANNA FARROW

PHOTOGRAPHS BY LIS PARSONS

spruce

An Hachette UK Company
www.hachette.co.uk

First published in Great Britain in 2012 by Spruce
a division of Octopus Publishing Group Ltd
Endeavour House, 189 Shaftesbury Avenue, London, WC2H 8JY
www.octopusbooks.co.uk
www.octopusbooksusa.com

Distributed in the US by Hachette Book Group USA
237 Park Avenue, New York NY 10017, USA

Distributed in Canada by Canadian Manda Group
165 Dufferin Street, Toronto, Ontario, Canada M6K 3H6

ISBN 13 978-1-84601-393-5
ISBN 10 1-84601-393-3

A CIP catalogue record for this book is available from the British Library

Printed and bound in China

10 9 8 7 6 5 4 3 2 1

This book includes cupcakes made with nuts. It is advisable for those
with known allergic reactions to nuts and those who may be potentially
vulnerable to these allergies, such as pregnant and nursing mothers, the
elderly, babies, and children, to avoid these items.

CONSULTANT PUBLISHER Sarah Ford
SENIOR EDITOR Leanne Bryan
COPY-EDITOR Nicole Foster
DESIGN MANAGER Eoghan O'Brien
DESIGNER theoakstudio.co.uk
PHOTOGRAPHER Lis Parsons
PRODUCTION MANAGER Katherine Hockley

CONTENTS

INTRODUCTION

Cupcakes are now as popular a choice for a wedding as a large, traditionally stacked fruitcake. Presented on decorative, tiered cupcake stands—whether cardboard, glass, or vintage—they look stunning, and each guest can take home their individual treat. The recipes in this book are all achievable—even by novice bakers—but do plan plenty of time for the more time-consuming decorations.

Rich fruit cupcakes can be made a couple of weeks in advance and fed with liqueur to keep them moist. Vanilla and rich chocolate cupcakes are best baked the day before decorating. Once frosted, they'll keep for another couple of days. If making any earlier, freeze in rigid containers, then thaw before decorating.

MAKES 24
PREPARATION TIME 15 minutes
COOKING TIME 25 minutes

2½ sticks (300 g) lightly salted butter, softened
1½ cups (300 g) superfine sugar
1 tablespoon vanilla bean paste or extract
5 eggs
2⅔ cups (325 g) self-rising flour
2 tablespoons milk

BASIC RECIPES

VANILLA CUPCAKES

Choose from this simple vanilla cupcake recipe or one of the variations below. Use two 12-cup muffin pans, baking those on the lower shelf of the oven for a few extra minutes if necessary. If making larger quantities, mix and bake them in separate batches.

Line two 12-cup muffin pans with paper baking cups and preheat the oven to 350°F (180°C).
    Put all the ingredients in a large mixing bowl and beat with a handheld electric mixer until smooth, creamy, and pale in color. Divide among the baking cups, filling them about two-thirds full, and bake for about 25 minutes until risen and just firm to the touch.
    Let stand in the pan for 5 minutes, then transfer to a cooling rack to cool.

FLAVOR VARIATIONS

Lemon: Omit the vanilla. Add the finely grated zest of 4 lemons and use lemon juice instead of milk.
Rose: Use 2 teaspoons rose water instead of the vanilla.
Almond: Replace ½ cup (50 g) flour with 1 cup (100 g) ground almonds and use 2 teaspoons almond extract instead of the vanilla.
White chocolate: Reduce the superfine sugar to 1 cup (200 g) and stir in 7 oz (200 g) melted white chocolate once mixed.

RICH CHOCOLATE CUPCAKES

Wedding cupcakes finished with dark chocolate decorations are usually combined with a rich chocolate cake base.

MAKES 24
PREPARATION TIME 15 minutes
COOKING TIME 25 minutes

1½ cups (125 g) unsweetened cocoa powder
1¼ cups (300 ml) boiling water
3 oz (75 g) semisweet chocolate, chopped
1¾ sticks (200 g) lightly salted butter, softened
1¾ cups (375 g) firmly packed light brown sugar
3 eggs
2½ cups (300 g) self-rising flour

Line two 12-cup muffin pans with paper baking cups (see chosen recipe if using colored baking cups) and preheat the oven to 350°F (180°C).

Put the cocoa powder in a heatproof bowl and whisk in the boiling water. Immediately add the chocolate and let cool, stirring frequently until smooth.

Beat the butter and sugar together with a handheld electric mixer to soften. Add the eggs, flour, and about a quarter of the chocolate mixture and beat well until smooth. Stir in the remaining chocolate mixture until evenly mixed.

Divide among the baking cups, filling them about two-thirds full, and bake for about 25 minutes until risen and just firm to the touch. Let stand in the pan for 5 minutes, then transfer to a cooling rack to cool.

RICH FRUIT CUPCAKES

Choose this recipe if you want a cupcake wedding cake but a rich and fruity cake base that can be topped with marzipan before decorating. Like a traditional rich fruitcake, the cupcakes can be pierced with a toothpick after cooling and drizzled with extra brandy, sherry, or orange liqueur, allowing for about ½ teaspoon for each cupcake.

MAKES 24
PREPARATION TIME 20 minutes, plus standing
COOKING TIME 40 minutes

4½ cups (800 g) mixed dried fruit
6 tablespoons brandy, sherry, or orange liqueur
2 sticks (225 g) lightly salted butter, softened
1 cup (225 g) firmly packed light brown sugar
4 eggs, beaten
2 cups (250 g) all-purpose flour
1½ tablespoons apple pie spice
1 cup (200 g) natural candied cherries, roughly chopped
1 cup (150 g) blanched almonds, chopped

Put the mixed dried fruit in a bowl and drizzle with the brandy, sherry, or orange liqueur. Cover and let stand for 2–3 hours, stirring once or twice until the liquid is absorbed.

Line two 12-cup muffin pans with paper baking cups (see chosen recipe if using colored baking cups) and preheat the oven to 350°F (180°C).

Cream together the butter and sugar until light and fluffy. Gradually beat in the eggs, a little at a time, adding a spoonful of the flour if the mixture starts to separate.

Sift the flour and spice into the bowl and stir in gently. Add the mixed dried fruits and any unabsorbed liquid, the cherries, and almonds, and stir in gently.

Divide among the baking cups, filling them almost full, and level the surface. Bake for about 35 minutes until risen and just firm to the touch. Let stand in the pan for 5 minutes, then transfer to a cooling rack to cool.

USEFUL TECHNIQUES

Coloring rolled fondant
Lightly knead the icing on a surface dusted with confectioners' sugar to soften it. Use a toothpick to dot a little food coloring onto the icing. Knead in until evenly colored then wrap tightly in plastic wrap until ready to use.

Covering cupcakes with rolled fondant
Roll out the icing on a surface dusted with confectioners' sugar to ⅛-inch (2.5-mm) thickness. Use a 3-inch (7-cm) cutter to press out circles. Lay the circles over the cupcakes, pressing them down gently around the edges.

Using a plunger cutter
Plunger cutters are perfect for cutting out a large quantity of tiny rolled-fondant flowers, hearts, or butterflies. Roll out the icing as thinly as possible so the shapes are fine and delicate. Push the cutter into the icing and lift away. Use the plunger spring to press out the shape onto a baking sheet or board lined with parchment paper. Let stand overnight, uncovered, to harden.

Covering cupcakes with frosting, ganache, or buttercream

Spoon a little of the frosting onto a cupcake and flatten down roughly with a knife. Use a small spatula to spread it from the center to the edges so the mixture covers the cupcake in a smooth layer in between the flutes of the baking cups. Some of the recipes build the frosting up in the center slightly to create a domed finish. Simply spoon more of the frosting onto the cake before smoothing it down to the edges.

Filling pastry bags

Use the same technique for filling paper, nylon, or plastic pastry bags. Remember to fit the tip first, then spoon in the icing or buttercream. Don't fill the bag more than two-thirds full or it'll ooze out of the end as you pipe. Twist nylon or plastic bags to seal, or fold over the ends if using a paper bag.

Piping lines and dots

Hold the bag at an angle of 45 degrees and gently squeeze the icing out, making sure you hold the sealed end with one hand, supporting the bag with the other. For lines, let the icing flow out in a steady stream, holding the bag slightly off the cake surface. For dots, hold the bag slightly more vertically and apply the smallest amount of pressure.

TRAILING FLOWERS

This cupcake design combines a classic theme with contemporary colors to create something a little different. Be careful to color the flower paste a soft silvery gray instead of a dark thundery one!

SERVES 48
PREPARATION AND DECORATING
TIME about 2¼ hours

1 quantity Vanilla Buttercream,
    see page 30
2 quantities (48) Vanilla Cupcakes,
    see page 4, baked in white or
    gray baking cups
Cream and black food coloring
2¾ lb (1.25 kg) white rolled fondant
Confectioners' sugar, for dusting
1 quantity Royal Icing, see page 18
26 yards (24 m) silvery gray organza
    ribbon, to decorate

TO PREPARE THE CUPCAKES Use a spatula to spread the buttercream over the cupcakes in a fairly smooth layer.

TO MAKE THE DECORATION Knead a little cream food coloring into 2 lb (1 kg) of the rolled fondant on a surface lightly dusted with confectioners' sugar until evenly colored. Wrap tightly in plastic wrap. Knead a little black food coloring into the remainder to color a soft shade of gray. Wrap tightly in plastic wrap.

Roll out half the cream-colored fondant on a surface dusted with confectioners' sugar to ⅛-inch (2.5-mm) thickness. Cut out circles using a 3-inch (7-cm) cutter. Use to cover the cupcakes, pressing the fondant down gently around the edges to cover the buttercream. Roll out the trimmings with the remaining cream fondant and use to cover the remaining cupcakes.

Reserve 3 tablespoons of the royal icing. Beat a little black coloring into the remainder until it's a similar shade of gray to the rolled fondant. Place in a small paper, nylon, or plastic pastry bag fitted with a writing tip. Use to pipe curved lines of icing all over the cupcakes.

TO FINISH Thinly roll out the gray fondant on a surface dusted with confectioners' sugar and cut out tiny flower shapes, using a ½-inch (1-cm) cutter (a plunger cutter is ideal, see page 6). Arrange the flowers on the cakes. Put the reserved royal icing in a paper, nylon, or plastic pastry bag fitted with a writing tip. Use to pipe dots into the centers of the flowers. Tie a length of ribbon around the base of each baking cup, to decorate, finishing with a bow.

SUGARED ALMOND CAKES

Prettily decorated with frosted flowers, these little cupcakes are perfect for a country-style family wedding. Choose sugared almonds to suit the colors planned for the wedding.

SERVES 24
PREPARATION AND DECORATING
TIME about 2¼ hours, plus setting

24 small edible flowers
1 egg white
Superfine sugar, for dusting
1 quantity (24) Vanilla Cupcakes, see page 4
½ cup (125 ml) sherry or orange-flavored liqueur (optional)
3¼ cups (400 g) confectioners' sugar, sifted
3–4 tablespoons lemon juice
72 sugared almonds
15 yards (14 m) white organza ribbon, to decorate

TO MAKE THE FROSTED FLOWERS Line a baking sheet with parchment paper. Make sure the flowers are clean and thoroughly dry before frosting. Put the egg white in a small bowl and beat lightly with a fork to break it up. Put plenty of superfine sugar in a separate bowl.

Take a flower and, using your fingers or a soft paintbrush, coat the petals on both sides with the egg white. Sprinkle plenty of superfine sugar over the flowers with your fingers, turning the flowers until evenly coated. Shake off the excess and place the flower on the lined sheet. Frost the remaining flowers and let stand overnight until dry and crisp. (If storing for any longer, place in an airtight container once completely dry, interleaving the layers with paper towels.)

TO PREPARE THE CUPCAKES Drizzle the cakes with the liqueur, if using. Mix the confectioners' sugar in a bowl with 2 tablespoons of the lemon juice. Gradually add the remaining lemon juice, stirring well with a wooden spoon until the icing holds its shape but is not difficult to spread—you may not need all the juice.

Spread the lemon-flavored icing over the cakes with a spatula and arrange 3 sugared almonds in the center of each. Place a frosted flower on top of each cake while the icing is still soft so they are held in place.

TO FINISH Tie a length of white organza ribbon around each baking cup, to decorate, finishing with a bow.

CONFETTI WEDDING CAKE

Delicate icing confetti, cascading down onto layers of cupcakes, looks incredibly pretty and effective.

SERVES 36
PREPARATION AND DECORATING
TIME 2½ hours, plus cooling and setting
COOKING TIME 25 minutes

Pink and yellow food coloring
1¾ lb (875 g) white rolled fondant
Confectioners' sugar, for dusting
1½ sticks (175 g) lightly salted butter, softened, plus extra for greasing
¾ cup plus 2 tablespoons (175 g) superfine sugar
3 eggs
1⅓ cups (175 g) self-rising flour
2 teaspoons vanilla extract
2 quantities Vanilla Buttercream, see page 30
6 tablespoons raspberry jelly
1 quantity (24) Vanilla Cupcakes, see page 4, baked in pale pink baking cups
½ quantity Royal Icing, see page 18
2 feet (60 cm) pale pink ribbon, ½ inch (1 cm) wide

TO MAKE THE DECORATION Knead a little pink food coloring into 3 oz (75 g) rolled fondant on a surface dusted with confectioners' sugar. Knead a little yellow coloring into 3 oz (75 g) fondant. Leave 3 oz (75 g) fondant white, then color the remainder with a tiny amount of pink coloring until the palest shade of pink. (Keep each fondant wrapped in plastic wrap until ready to use.)

Line two large baking sheets with parchment paper. Thinly roll out the pale yellow fondant on a surface dusted with confectioners' sugar and cut out a mixture of confetti shapes, using small heart, horseshoe, bell, and flower cutters. Reroll the trimmings to make extras. Repeat with the white and smaller quantity of pink fondant to make more shapes. Let harden overnight.

TO MAKE THE LARGE CAKE Grease and line the bottom of three 6-inch (15-cm) layer cake pans and preheat the oven to 350°F (180°C).

Beat the butter, superfine sugar, eggs, flour, and vanilla in a bowl with a handheld electric mixer until pale and creamy. Divide among the pans and level the surfaces. Bake for 20–25 minutes until risen and just firm. Transfer to a cooling rack to cool.

Sandwich the cakes together using 3 tablespoons buttercream and 3 tablespoons jelly between each layer. Place on a 6-inch (15-cm) cake card. Using a spatula, spread the top and sides of the cake with a thin layer of buttercream.

Roll out the larger quantity of pink fondant to a 12-inch (30-cm) circle on a surface dusted with confectioners' sugar. Lift the fondant over the cake and ease around the sides to fit. Smooth out flat and trim off the excess around the base with a knife.

TO FINISH Put half the remaining buttercream in a large pastry bag fitted with a large star tip. Decorate the tops of the cupcakes, refilling the bag when necessary.

Put the royal icing into a small paper, nylon, or plastic pastry bag fitted with a writing tip. Wrap the ribbon around the bottom of the large cake, securing with a dot of royal icing. Secure confetti shapes to the large cake with royal icing so that they look like they're falling down the sides. Scatter more confetti over the cupcakes.

Arrange the cakes on a tiered cake stand so the large cake sits on the top tier and the cupcakes on the lower tiers. Alternatively, use an 8–9-inch (20–23-cm) stand and assemble the cupcakes on the surface or on a large, flat plate beneath.

SPRING WEDDING

Decorate these cakes up to two days in advance. It's easiest to arrange the rolled fondant over the cakes while the buttercream is still soft.

SERVES 48
PREPARATION AND DECORATING
TIME about 1½ hours

2 quantities Vanilla Buttercream,
  see page 30
2 quantities (48) White Chocolate
  Cupcakes, see page 4, baked in
  pale green or yellow baking cups
Green food coloring
14 oz (400 g) white rolled fondant
Confectioners' sugar, for dusting

TO PREPARE THE CUPCAKES Put 3 tablespoons buttercream in a small paper, nylon, or plastic pastry bag fitted with a writing tip. Using a spatula, spread the remaining buttercream over the cupcakes in a smooth layer.

TO MAKE THE DECORATION Knead a little green food coloring into half the rolled fondant on a surface dusted with confectioners' sugar until a very delicate, pastel shade. Thinly roll out half the pale green fondant on a surface dusted with confectioners' sugar (keeping the remainder tightly wrapped in plastic wrap), and cut into thin strips about ¼ inch (5 mm) wide. Press four strips, evenly spaced, onto each cake. Trim off the excess with a sharp knife. Use the trimmings and the remaining pale green fondant to cover the remaining cupcakes.

TO FINISH Thinly roll out the remaining white rolled fondant and cut out small flower shapes using a ½-inch (1-cm) flower cutter (a plunger cutter is ideal, see page 6). Arrange the flowers on the cupcakes between the green strips. Use the buttercream in the pastry bag to pipe small dots into the centers of the flowers.

CUPCAKE HEARTS

Use either heart-shaped silicone or metal cupcake cups or a heart-shaped silicone cake pan for these cakes. You'll need to bake in batches, depending on how many pan sections or cups you have.

SERVES 24
PREPARATION AND DECORATING
TIME about 2 hours, plus cooling
COOKING TIME 25 minutes
per batch

Butter, for greasing (optional)
1 quantity Almond Cupcakes batter, see page 4
½ cup (125 ml) almond liqueur (optional)
⅔ cup (200 g) apricot jam
14 oz (400 g) marzipan
Confectioners' sugar, for dusting
Cream food coloring
3¼ lb (1.5 kg) white rolled fondant
½ quantity Royal Icing, see page 18
Plenty of pearl dragées

TO MAKE THE HEART CAKES Preheat the oven to 350°F (180°C). Place cupcake cups on a baking sheet, and grease the cups if using metal ones. Spoon the cupcake batter into the molds so they're about two-thirds full. Bake for 20–25 minutes until risen and just firm to the touch. Let stand in the molds for 5 minutes, then loosen the edges and invert onto a cooling rack to cool. Cook the remaining batches in the same way.

Trim off the risen centers of the cakes, if necessary, so they sit flat when inverted. Drizzle the cakes with the liqueur, if using.

TO DECORATE THE CAKES Press the jam through a sieve into a small saucepan and add 2 tablespoons water. Heat gently until syrupy, then brush the glaze over the cakes. Roll out the marzipan to ¼-inch (5-mm) thickness on a surface lightly dusted with confectioners' sugar and cut out heart shapes the same size as the cakes. (The easiest way to do this is to draw around one of the cups or pan sections, cut it out, and use as a template.) Place a heart on top of each cake, rerolling the trimmings to make extras.

Knead a little cream food coloring into the rolled fondant on a surface dusted with confectioners' sugar to make a pale ivory color. Thinly roll out 2 oz (50 g) of the fondant (keeping the remainder tightly wrapped in plastic wrap) and use to cover one of the hearts. Ease the icing around the sides, trimming off the excess around the base. Cover the remaining cakes in the same way. Press a 1¼-inch (3-cm) heart-shaped cutter into the top of each cake to leave a heart-shaped impression.

TO FINISH Color the royal icing with a little cream food coloring and put in a small paper, nylon, or plastic pastry bag fitted with a writing tip. Use to pipe an outline over the impressed heart shapes. Press the pearl dragées into the piping to decorate.

STACKED CUPCAKES WITH LIMES, CHILIES, AND ROSES

Although these cakes are undecorated, the surrounding herbs, fruits, and flowers combine to create a stunning display. Replace the rich fruitcakes with a flavored cake if you prefer.

SERVES 48
PREPARATION AND DECORATING
    TIME about 1½ hours

⅔ cup (200 g) apricot jam

2 tablespoons brandy or orange liqueur

2 quantities (48) Rich Fruit Cupcakes, see page 5, baked in white baking cups

1 lb 2 oz (500 g) marzipan

Confectioners' sugar, for dusting

2 quantities Royal Icing, see below

TO DECORATE

Plenty of sprigs of bay leaves

10–12 small fresh limes

About 20 green chilies

Plenty of white or ivory roses

TO PREPARE THE CUPCAKES Press the apricot jam through a sieve into a small bowl and beat in the brandy or liqueur, if using, or 2 tablespoons water to make a glaze. Brush the glaze over the cakes.

Roll out the marzipan to ⅛-inch (2.5-mm) thickness on a surface dusted with confectioners' sugar and cut out circles using a 2-inch (5-cm) cutter. Place a circle of marzipan on each cake, rerolling the trimmings, if necessary, to make enough.

Using a spatula, spread the royal icing over the cupcakes.

TO FINISH Arrange the cupcakes on a tiered stand, leaving a little space in between each. Tuck bay leaves around the cakes, then add the limes, some halved, chilies, and roses. To make the roses stay fresh-looking for several hours, cut the stalks down to about 3 inches (7 cm) and enclose the cut ends in moistened cotton balls. Seal with plastic wrap before tucking the flowers between the cupcakes, hiding the cut ends under the other decorations.

ROYAL ICING

Royal icing can be spread over cupcakes or used for piping decorations. It keeps well for several days in the refrigerator if you seal the surface with plastic wrap to stop a crust from forming. Beat well before using.

PREPARATION TIME
    10 minutes

2 egg whites

About 3¾ cups (475 g) confectioners' sugar

Put the egg whites in a large bowl with a little of the confectioners' sugar and beat well with a handheld electric mixer until smooth. Gradually beat in the remaining sugar until the icing forms soft peaks when the beaters are lifted from the bowl. Cover the surface with plastic wrap until ready to use.

BOW CAKES

To make these cakes, use a 16-section cake pan with each section measuring 2 inches (5 cm) in diameter and 2 inches (5 cm) deep. They are more time-consuming to make than cupcakes but can be decorated a week in advance and stored in a cool place.

SERVES 24
PREPARATION AND DECORATING
TIME about 3 hours, plus cooling
COOKING TIME 1 hour 10 minutes

Butter, for greasing
1 quantity Rich Fruit Cupcakes batter, see page 5
²⁄₃ cup (200 g) apricot jam
3 tablespoons brandy or orange liqueur (optional)
1 lb 10 oz (750 g) marzipan
Confectioners' sugar, for dusting
8 cups (1 kg) fondant sugar
Blue and black food coloring
1 lb 10 oz (750 g) white rolled fondant

TO MAKE THE CAKES Preheat the oven to 350°F (180°C). Grease and line the sections of a 16-sectioned cake pan containing 2-inch (5-cm) round mini cake rings. Spoon the cake batter into the sections and level the surfaces so each section is almost filled. (You'll have enough batter left to make another eight cakes.) Bake for 35 minutes or until the cakes feel just firm and a toothpick inserted into one comes out clean. Let cool in the pan, then bake the remaining batter in the same way, using only eight of the rings.

TO PREPARE THE CAKES FOR DECORATION Press the apricot jam through a sieve into a small bowl and beat in the liqueur, if using, or 3 tablespoons water to make a glaze. Brush the glaze over the tops and sides of the cakes.

Roll out half the marzipan to ⅛-inch (2.5-mm) thickness on a surface dusted with confectioners' sugar and cut out circles using a 2-inch (5-cm) cutter. Press a circle onto the top of each cake. Reroll the trimmings with the remaining marzipan and cut out rectangles large enough to wrap around the sides of the cakes.

Put the fondant sugar in a bowl and beat in enough cold water (you'll probably need about ²⁄₃ cup/150 ml) to produce a smooth consistency that thickly coats the back of a metal spoon. Place the cakes on two cooling racks and spoon over the icing until coated, smoothing it around the sides with a spatula.

TO MAKE THE DECORATION Knead blue food coloring and a dash of black coloring into the rolled fondant on a surface dusted with confectioners' sugar. Thinly roll out a quarter of the fondant (keeping the rest tightly wrapped in plastic wrap) and cut into 1-inch (2.5-cm) wide strips. Lay the strips over the cakes, trimming off the excess at the bottoms.

Roll out more fondant, cut out more strips, then cut across into 2-inch (5-cm) rectangles. Bend the rectangles over and pinch the ends together to shape the loops of a bow. Position two loops on top of each cake, leaving a small space in between and securing with a dampened paintbrush. Cut the last strips of fondant into ⅜-inch (8-mm) squares and place between the loops to shape the knots.

COUNTRY WEDDING

These little cakes are perfect for an informal wedding. Ice and add the lavender bundles the day before the wedding.

SERVES 48
PREPARATION AND DECORATING
TIME about 1½ hours

8 cups (1 kg) confectioners' sugar
½–⅔ cup (125–150 ml) lemon juice
Lilac food coloring
2 quantities (48) Vanilla Cupcakes,
    see page 4, baked in a mixture
    of white and lilac baking cups
Plenty of lavender sprigs
15 yards (14 m) fine lilac ribbon,
    cut into 11-inch (28-cm) lengths

TO MAKE THE ICING Mix the confectioners' sugar with enough lemon juice to make a smooth glaze that is not quite thick enough to hold its shape when the spoon is lifted from the bowl. (Add the lemon juice cautiously once nearly mixed so you don't overthin the icing.) Stir in a little lilac food coloring.

TO FINISH Spread the icing over the cakes with a spatula so that it just starts to run over the sides of the cakes. (If it's too runny, work in a little more confectioners' sugar; if it's too thick to spread, add a dash more lemon juice.)

Tie the lavender sprigs together in twos with the ribbon and press gently onto the icing.

PINK ROSE

Make these cupcakes as delicately or vividly colored as you prefer. You'll need a lot of fondant roses but they're very easy and quick to make and keep well for several weeks. Let harden overnight on the parchment paper before storing in an airtight container.

SERVES 48
PREPARATION AND DECORATING
TIME about 4 hours, plus setting

Pink food coloring
14 oz (400 g) white rolled fondant
Confectioners' sugar, for dusting
2 quantities (48) Rose Cupcakes,
  see page 4, baked in white, pale
  pink, or deep pink baking cups

FROSTING

2¼ lb (1 kg) mascarpone cheese
7 tablespoons (100 g) unsalted
  butter, softened
4 cups (500 g) confectioners' sugar
2 tablespoons lemon juice
Pink food coloring

TO MAKE THE ROSES Line two or three baking sheets with parchment paper. Knead pink food coloring into the rolled fondant on a surface dusted with confectioners' sugar until the desired shade of pink.

Take a ball of the fondant, about the size of a pea, and roll it under your fingers until about 1½ inches (3.5 cm) long. (Keep the rest of the fondant tightly wrapped in plastic wrap while not in use.) Use a little confectioners' sugar to dust your fingers and the surface if the fondant is sticky. Flatten the strip until about ½ inch (1 cm) wide and then roll it up to resemble a simple rosebud shape, pinching the fondant around the base so the rose opens out slightly. Slice off the base and transfer to a lined sheet while you make the remainder. You'll need about 430 in all.

TO MAKE THE FROSTING Beat together the mascarpone and butter until smooth. Add the confectioners' sugar and lemon juice and beat well until evenly combined. Beat in a little pink food coloring until the frosting is the required shade of pink.

TO FINISH Using a spatula, spread the frosting over the tops of the cupcakes, swirling with the edge to add texture. Gently press the roses into the frosting.

FROSTED FLOWER

Fresh flowers look stunning sealed in a frosting of sugar, which preserves their color and shape for up to several weeks. Use any edible, seasonal flowers. Primroses and violas look pretty for the spring, while small roses can be used throughout the summer.

SERVES 48
PREPARATION AND DECORATING
TIME about 2¼ hours, plus setting

48 small edible flowers
2 egg whites
Superfine sugar, for dusting
12 cups (1.5 kg) fondant sugar
2 quantities (48) Almond Cupcakes, see page 4, baked in white or pastel baking cups
About 20 yards (18 m) colored ribbon (optional)

TO MAKE THE FROSTED FLOWERS Line two baking sheets with parchment paper. Make sure the flowers are clean and thoroughly dry before frosting. Put the egg whites in a small bowl and beat lightly with a fork to break them up. Put plenty of superfine sugar in a separate bowl.

Take a flower and, using your fingers or a soft paintbrush, coat the petals on both sides with the egg white. If using roses, open out the petals with your fingers so you can get between the petals to coat them—if the centers of the roses are tightly packed, you won't be able to coat them entirely. Sprinkle plenty of sugar over the flowers with your fingers, turning the flowers until evenly coated. Shake off the excess and place the flower on the lined sheets. Frost the remaining flowers and let stand overnight until dry and crisp. (If storing for any longer, place in an airtight container once completely dry, interleaving the layers with paper towels.)

TO MAKE THE ICING Put the fondant sugar in a bowl and beat in enough cold water to produce a smooth consistency that thickly coats the back of a metal spoon. You'll probably need up to 14 tablespoons water in all, but add it cautiously toward the end so you don't make the icing too thin. Spread the icing over the cakes with a spatula, letting a little icing fall slightly over the sides of the baking cups. (If the icing is too thin and runs quickly down the sides, beat in a little more fondant sugar.)

TO FINISH Arrange the flowers while the icing is still soft so they're held in place. Tie a length of ribbon around each baking cup, if using, to decorate.

WHITE HEART

Perfect for a traditional white wedding, these cupcakes look really impressive on a tiered cake stand. They can be decorated up to a week in advance and stored in airtight containers.

SERVES 48
PREPARATION AND DECORATING
TIME about 2¼ hours, plus setting

10 oz (300 g) white rolled fondant

Confectioners' sugar, for dusting

⅔ cup (200 g) apricot jam

2 tablespoons brandy or orange liqueur (optional)

2 quantities (48) Rich Fruit Cupcakes, see page 5, baked in white baking cups

1 lb (500 g) marzipan

2 quantities Royal Icing, see page 18

About 20 yards (18 m) colored ribbon (optional)

TO MAKE THE HEARTS Line two baking sheets with parchment paper. Roll out the fondant to ⅛-inch (2.5-mm) thickness on a surface lightly dusted with confectioners' sugar. Cut out heart shapes using a ¾–1¼-inch (2–3-cm) heart-shaped cutter and transfer to the parchment paper. Make at least 50 hearts in total so you have a few spares in case of any breakages. Let harden overnight.

TO PREPARE THE CUPCAKES Press the apricot jam through a sieve into a small bowl and beat in the brandy or liqueur, if using, or 2 tablespoons water to make a glaze. Brush the glaze over the cupcakes.

Roll out the marzipan to ⅛-inch (2.5-mm) thickness on a surface dusted with confectioners' sugar and cut out circles using a 2-inch (5-cm) cutter. Place a circle of marzipan on each cake, rerolling the trimmings to make enough.

TO FINISH Put 2 tablespoons of the royal icing in a small paper, nylon, or plastic pastry bag fitted with a writing tip. Use to outline the edges of the hearts.

Spread the remaining royal icing over the cupcakes with a spatula. Lift the hearts from the paper and gently press onto the centers of the cupcakes. If the hearts won't stay vertical, push a wooden toothpick into each cake behind the heart to support it, twisting it out carefully once the icing has set. Tie ribbon around the cakes to finish, if desired.

PINK AND PRETTY

Soft and delicate, this cupcake design is particularly suited to an informal summer wedding. The simple decoration is easy and achievable on the day of the wedding.

SERVES 48
PREPARATION AND DECORATION
TIME about 1½ hours

Pink food coloring
2 quantities Vanilla Buttercream, see below
2 quantities (48) Almond Cupcakes, see page 4, baked in pink baking cups
Plenty of pink heart sugar sprinkles
Plenty of sugar pearls

TO PREPARE THE CUPCAKES Beat a little pink food coloring into the buttercream to a very pale shade of pink. Using a spatula, spread a little buttercream over the cupcakes in a fairly smooth layer.

TO FINISH Put half the remaining buttercream in a paper, nylon, or plastic pastry bag fitted with a small star tip. Use to pipe shells around the edges of the cupcakes. Refill the bag (or use a new one if using paper) and pipe the remaining buttercream.

While the buttercream is still soft, scatter pink heart sugar sprinkles and sugar pearls around the edges of the cakes so they fall mainly over the piping.

VANILLA BUTTERCREAM

Buttercream is used for spreading over cupcakes, sandwiching layers together, and for piping. It keeps well for several days in the refrigerator stored in an airtight container.

PREPARATION TIME
10 minutes

2 sticks (250 g) unsalted butter, softened
3 cups (375 g) confectioners' sugar
1 tablespoon vanilla extract or vanilla bean paste
1 tablespoon boiling water

Put the butter, confectioners' sugar, and vanilla in a large bowl and beat with a handheld electric mixer until very pale in color. Add the boiling water and beat again until light and fluffy.

FLAVOR VARIATIONS
Lemon: Add the finely grated zest of 2 lemons and use 3 tablespoons lemon juice instead of the vanilla and boiling water.
Rose: Omit the vanilla and add 2 teaspoons rose extract.
Chocolate: Add ¾ cup plus 2 tablespoons (75 g) unsweetened cocoa powder when beating and stir in 7 oz (200 g) melted semisweet chocolate until evenly combined.

BRIDE AND GROOM

These fun cupcakes feature bride and groom cake "toppers."

SERVES 48
PREPARATION AND DECORATING
TIME about 3½ hours

⅔ cup (200 g) apricot jam
2 tablespoons brandy or orange
  liqueur (optional)
2 quantities (48) Almond Cupcakes,
  see page 4, half baked in white
  or pale pink baking cups, half
  in black baking cups
1 lb 2 oz (500 g) marzipan
Confectioners' sugar, for dusting
2 quantities Royal Icing, see page 18
Black and pink food coloring
2¼ lb (1 kg) white rolled fondant

TO PREPARE THE CUPCAKES Press the apricot jam through a sieve into a small bowl and beat in the brandy or liqueur, if using, or 2 tablespoons water to make a glaze. Brush the glaze over the cakes.

Roll out the marzipan to ⅛-inch (2.5-mm) thickness on a surface dusted with confectioners' sugar and cut out circles using a 2-inch (5-cm) cutter. Place a circle of marzipan on each cake, rerolling the trimmings to make enough.

Reserve 6 tablespoons of the royal icing. Use the remainder to cover the cupcakes in a thin layer, spreading the icing fairly smooth with a spatula.

TO MAKE THE DECORATION Knead black food coloring into 1 lb (500 g) of the rolled fondant on a surface dusted with confectioners' sugar. Knead a little pink food coloring into an additional 3½ oz (100 g) of the fondant, leaving the remainder white. Wrap each color tightly in plastic wrap until ready to use.

Thinly roll out half the black fondant and cut circles using a 3-inch (7-cm) cutter. Cut a deep "v" shape from one side so the points reach the centers of the circles and secure the shapes on the cupcakes in the black baking cups. Reroll the trimmings with the remaining black fondant and use to cover the rest of the black cakes.

Thinly roll out half the white fondant and cut out circles with the same cutter. From each circle cut away three curved sides to leave a bodice shape. Secure on the cupcakes in the pink or white baking cups. Reroll the trimmings with the remaining fondant to cover the rest of the cakes.

TO FINISH Color half the reserved royal icing black and put in a small paper, nylon, or plastic pastry bag fitted with a writing tip. Put the remaining royal icing in a separate pastry bag fitted with a writing tip. Use the white icing to pipe outlines around each bodice on the bride cakes, then fill in the centers with small dots. Use the black icing to pipe collars and buttons onto the groom cakes.

Thinly roll and cut out "cravat" shapes from the pink fondant and secure in place, finishing with piped lines of black icing. Roll thin lengths of pink fondant under your fingers then twist two lengths together to shape necklaces. Press gently in place on the bride cakes. Use the remaining pink fondant to make flowers for bouquets and boutonnieres using a ½-inch (1-cm) plunger cutter (see page 6). Secure in place with a dampened paintbrush and pipe dots of white icing into the centers.

MINI WEDDING CAKES

Shaping and decorating these cakes takes more time than regular cupcakes, but they're perfect for the more creative cook! Make the cakes a day in advance of decorating because they'll be so much easier to shape.

SERVES 16
PREPARATION AND DECORATING TIME 4–5 hours, plus cooling
COOKING TIME 35 minutes

Butter, for greasing
1 quantity Lemon Cupcake batter, see page 4
⅔ cup (200 g) lemon curd
4½ lb (2 kg) white rolled fondant
Confectioners' sugar, for dusting

TO MAKE THE LARGE CAKES Preheat the oven to 350°F (180°C). Grease and line the bottom and sides of a 9-inch (23-cm) and a 7-inch (18-cm) square cake pan. Spoon two-thirds of the cake batter into the large pan and the remainder into the small pan. Level the surfaces and bake in the preheated oven, placing the larger cake on the upper shelf and the smaller one on the lower shelf, for 30–35 minutes until risen and just firm to the touch. Transfer to a cooling rack to cool.

TO PREPARE THE MINI CAKES Cut out 16 circles from the larger cake using a 2-inch (5-cm) cutter. Cut out 16 circles from the smaller cake using a 1½-inch (3.5-cm) cutter. Spread a little lemon curd over the tops of the larger cakes and press a smaller cake gently on top. Spread the remaining lemon curd over the small cakes and almost down to the bottoms of the large ones.

Roll out 2½ oz (65 g) of the rolled fondant to a 5-inch (12-cm) circle on a surface lightly dusted with confectioners' sugar. (Keep the remainder tightly wrapped in plastic wrap.) Position over one cake and fit it around the sides, easing the fondant as smoothly as you can around the top tier, then around the bottom tier. Try to eliminate any folds around the sides, though some of these can be covered by the decoration. Trim off the excess around the bottom and cover the remaining cakes in the same way.

TO MAKE THE DECORATION Roll out the fondant as thinly as you can and cut out strips 3 x ¼ inch (7 cm x 5 mm). Dampen the underside of each strip with a paintbrush and secure the strips vertically around the cakes so the ends meet on top. Cut smaller strips measuring 1¼ x ¼ inch (3 cm x 5 mm). Bend into loops and use these to decorate the tops of the cakes, securing the loops with a dampened paintbrush and allowing for nine loops per cake.

FLOWER POWER

Colorful and bold, this cake design is great for an informal, relaxed wedding. Use several small flower cutters in different sizes. Plunger cutters are ideal (see page 6).

SERVES 48
PREPARATION AND DECORATING
TIME about 1½ hours

2 quantities Lemon Buttercream, see page 30

2 quantities (48) Lemon Cupcakes, see page 4, baked in a mixture of pink, green, and yellow baking cups

14 oz (400 g) white rolled fondant

Pink, green, and yellow food coloring

Confectioners' sugar, for dusting

Pink, green, and yellow mini candy-coated chocolates

TO PREPARE THE CUPCAKES Reserve 6 tablespoons of the buttercream and spread the remainder over the cupcakes in a fairly smooth layer using a spatula.

TO MAKE THE DECORATION Divide the rolled fondant into three pieces. Knead a little pink food coloring into one piece, green into another, and yellow into the remainder, working on a surface dusted with confectioners' sugar. (Keep each color tightly wrapped in plastic wrap until ready to use.) Roll out the pink fondant on a surface dusted with confectioners' sugar. The fondant should be rolled as thinly as possible without tearing. Cut out different-size flower shapes and place in the centers of the cupcakes in the pink baking cups. (You'll need about six to eight flowers on each cake.) Reroll the trimmings, if necessary, to make enough. Use the green and yellow fondant in the same way to cover the remaining cakes.

TO FINISH Put the reserved buttercream in a paper, nylon, or plastic pastry bag fitted with a writing tip and use to pipe dots into the centers of the small flowers. Pipe more dots into the larger flowers and press small candy-coated chocolates into the centers.

FILIGREE HEARTS

Red hearts are always appropriate for a wedding but you can easily change them to a color, pastel or otherwise, that links better with the colors planned for the wedding.

SERVES 48
PREPARATION AND DECORATING
TIME about 2 hours, plus setting

Red food coloring
7 oz (200 g) white rolled fondant
Confectioners' sugar, for dusting
½ quantity Royal Icing, see page 18
3 quantities Lemon Buttercream,
   see page 30
2 quantities (48) Lemon Cupcakes,
   see page 4, baked in white
   baking cups

TO MAKE THE HEARTS Line two baking sheets with parchment paper. Knead red food coloring into the rolled fondant to a deep shade of red on a surface dusted with confectioners' sugar. Roll out the fondant to ⅛-inch (2.5-mm) thickness. Cut out heart shapes using a 1¼-inch (3-cm) heart-shaped cutter and transfer to the parchment paper. Make at least 50 hearts so you have several spares in case of any breakages.

Color the royal icing deep red and put in a small paper, nylon, or plastic pastry bag fitted with a writing tip. Use to pipe fine wiggly lines all over the hearts. Let harden overnight.

TO FINISH Put half the buttercream in a large nylon or plastic pastry bag fitted with a large star tip. Use to pipe shells, starting at the edges of the cupcakes and trailing off in the centers. Refill the bag with the remaining buttercream to pipe the remainder.

Lift the hearts from the paper and rest them gently on the cupcakes.

WINTER WEDDING

Simple to make but so eye catching, these cupcakes are just right for a midwinter wedding. Frost and decorate the cupcakes the day before the wedding. For the best effect, arrange the cupcakes on a glass, white, or silver tiered stand.

SERVES 48
PREPARATION AND DECORATING TIME about 2 hours

2 quantities (48) Almond Cupcakes, see page 4, baked in white baking cups
¾ cup (200 ml) almond liqueur (optional)
Seeds of 6 pomegranates
16 egg whites
6¾ cups (850 g) confectioners' sugar
2 teaspoons cream of tartar
Pinch of salt
Plenty of silver dragées, preferably in 3 sizes

TO PREPARE THE CUPCAKES Pierce each cupcake several times with a toothpick and drizzle with the almond liqueur, if using. Pat the pomegranate seeds dry on plenty of paper towels.

TO MAKE THE FROSTING Prepare the frosting in two batches. Put half the egg whites, half the confectioners' sugar, half the cream of tartar, and a pinch of salt in a large heatproof mixing bowl and rest the bowl over a saucepan of gently simmering water, making sure the bottom of the bowl does not rest in the water. Beat with a handheld electric mixer for about 8 minutes or until the frosting starts to thicken. Remove the bowl from the heat and beat for 5 minutes more or until the mixture has a softly peaking meringuelike consistency that holds its shape.

TO FINISH Pile the frosting onto half the cupcakes and spread with a spatula, doming the frosting up a little in the centers. Sprinkle with pomegranate seeds and silver dragées. Cover the remaining cupcakes in the same way using a second batch of frosting.

FLOWER GARDEN

These little celebration cakes are so easy and effective; perfect for a child to make for a small, informal wedding.

SERVES 24
PREPARATION AND DECORATING
TIME about 1½ hours, plus setting

10 oz (300 g) white rolled fondant
Blue, pink, and lilac food coloring
Confectioners' sugar, for dusting
1 quantity Rose Buttercream,
    see page 30
1 quantity (24) Rose Cupcakes,
    see page 4, baked in blue, pink,
    or lilac baking cups

TO MAKE THE DECORATION Line two baking sheets with parchment paper. Divide the rolled fondant into three pieces. Knead a little blue food coloring into one piece, pink into another, and lilac into the remainder, working on a surface dusted with confectioners' sugar. (Keep the colored fondants tightly wrapped in plastic wrap until ready to use.)

Roll out the blue fondant on a surface dusted with confectioners' sugar. Cut out small flower shapes using a 1-inch (2.5-cm) flower cutter. Transfer to a lined sheet. Repeat with the remaining colors until you have about 130 flowers. Let stand for several hours or overnight to harden. (Once hard, they can be stored in an airtight container, layers interleaved with paper towels, for up to two weeks.)

TO PREPARE THE CUPCAKES Put 4 tablespoons of the buttercream in a small paper, nylon, or plastic pastry bag fitted with a writing tip. Using a spatula, spread the cupcakes with the remaining buttercream.

TO FINISH Arrange the fondant flowers on top of the cupcakes. Pipe seven or eight buttercream dots into the center of each flower.

CHRISTMAS WEDDING

These cakes are very simply decorated but could have fresh cranberries and silver candied chocolates scattered around them once arranged on a cake stand to add a splash of festive color. Because they're made of rich fruitcake and totally covered with fondant, they can be made and decorated up to two weeks in advance and kept in a cool place until the wedding.

SERVES 48
PREPARATION AND DECORATING
TIME about 1¾ hours

⅔ cup (200 g) apricot jam
2 tablespoons brandy or orange liqueur (optional)
2 quantities (48) Rich Fruit Cupcakes, see page 5, baked in red or white baking cups
1 lb 2 oz (500 g) marzipan
Confectioners' sugar, for dusting
2¼ lb (1 kg) white rolled fondant
½ quantity Royal Icing, see page 18
26 yards (24 metres) fine red ribbon, to decorate

TO PREPARE THE CUPCAKES Press the apricot jam through a sieve into a small bowl and beat in the brandy or liqueur, if using, or 2 tablespoons water to make a glaze. Brush the glaze over the cakes.

Roll out the marzipan to ⅛-inch (2.5-mm) thickness on a surface dusted with confectioners' sugar and cut out circles using a 2-inch (5-cm) round cutter. Place a circle of marzipan on each cake, rerolling the trimmings to make enough.

TO DECORATE THE CUPCAKES Thinly roll out half the white rolled fondant on a surface dusted with confectioners' sugar (keeping the remainder tightly wrapped in plastic wrap). Cut out circles using a 3-inch (7-cm) cutter. Position on the cakes, smoothing the circles down around the edges. Reroll the trimmings with the remaining fondant to cover the remaining cupcakes.

Put the royal icing in a paper, nylon, or plastic pastry bag fitted with a writing tip and use to pipe small dots, about ½ inch (1 cm) apart, all over the white fondant to decorate.

TO FINISH Cut the ribbon into 20-inch (50-cm) lengths and tie a length around each baking cup, to decorate, finishing with a bow.

BOLLYWOOD CAKES

Add a splash of vibrant color to your wedding with these quirky cupcakes, which can be decorated several days in advance.

SERVES 48
PREPARATION AND DECORATING
TIME about 2½ hours

2 quantities (48) Rose Cupcakes,
  see page 4, baked in bright blue,
  pink, and orange baking cups
2 quantities Rose Buttercream,
  see page 30
2¾ lb (1.25 kg) white rolled fondant
Confectioners' sugar, for dusting
Blue, pink, orange, and yellow food
  coloring
½ quantity Royal Icing, see page 18
Plenty of gold dragées

TO PREPARE THE CUPCAKES Use a spatula to spread the cupcakes with a thick layer of buttercream, doming it up slightly in the center.

TO MAKE THE DECORATION Divide the rolled fondant into three pieces. Working on a surface dusted with confectioners' sugar, knead blue food coloring into one piece, pink into the second, and orange into the third. Wrap the colored fondants tightly in plastic wrap until ready to use.

Roll out the blue fondant to ⅛-inch (2.5-mm) thickness on a surface dusted with confectioners' sugar. Cut out circles using a 3-inch (7-cm) cutter and place the circles on the cupcakes in the blue baking cups, pressing the fondant down gently around the edges to cover the buttercream. Use the pink fondant to cover the cakes in pink cups and the orange for those in orange cups.

TO FINISH Beat yellow food coloring into the royal icing and put in a small paper, nylon, or plastic pastry bag fitted with a writing tip. Use to pipe swirling lines over the cupcakes. Fill any large gaps between the piping by positioning the gold dragées, securing them in place with dots of icing from the bag.

IVORY ROSE

Making chocolate roses is time-consuming but so rewarding. Once made, they'll keep in an airtight container for a couple of weeks so you can gradually build up the required amount.

SERVES 48
PREPARATION AND DECORATING
   TIME about 4½ hours, plus cooling

5½ lb (2.5 kg) white chocolate
   modeling paste
Confectioners' sugar, for dusting
2 cups (450 ml) heavy cream
2 teaspoons rose water
1 lb (450 g) white chocolate,
   chopped
2 quantities (48) Rose Cupcakes,
   see page 4, baked in black, pink,
   or white baking cups

TO MAKE THE ROSES Knead a small quantity of modeling paste in your fingers to soften it and make it pliable. Break off a grape-size piece and shape it into a cone, pressing the thick end down on the surface. Pinch the cone in the center to make a waist. Take a small ball of paste, about the size of a large pea, and press it between your thumb and finger to shape a paper-thin petal. (Dust your hands lightly with confectioners' sugar if they become sticky.) Wrap around the cone into a tight curl. This will form the center of the rose. Shape another slightly larger petal and wrap it around the cone. Continue layering up the petals, making each one slightly larger than the previous and opening them out as you work. You'll need 9–10 petals for each rose. Slice the rose off the bottom (so about half the cone is left) and transfer to a baking sheet lined with parchment paper. Rebuild the cone shape and use the remaining modeling paste to make more roses in the same way until you have 48 in all.

TO MAKE THE GANACHE Heat half the cream with the rose water in a saucepan until bubbling up around the edges but not boiling. Stir in the chopped white chocolate and transfer to a bowl. Let cool, stirring occasionally until the chocolate has melted and the mixture is completely cold. Stir in the remaining cream and chill until thickened.

TO FINISH Before spreading the ganache check its consistency. If it doesn't hold its shape when stirred, beat very lightly with a handheld electric mixer until it just holds its shape. Spread over the cupcakes using a spatula, and press a chocolate rose down gently onto each. Store in a cool place for up to 24 hours.

WEDDING PACKAGES

Dark and delicious, these gooey chocolate treats are finished with beautiful molded bows and red heart shapes.

SERVES 48
PREPARATION AND DECORATING
TIME about 2½ hours, plus cooling

2 quantities (48) Rich Chocolate Cupcakes, see page 5, baked in brown baking cups

About 1 cup (240 ml) almond or hazelnut liqueur (optional)

3 cups (750 ml) heavy cream

3 tablespoons confectioners' sugar, plus extra for dusting

1 lb 10 oz (750 g) semisweet chocolate, chopped

1 lb 10 oz (750 g) chocolate-flavored rolled fondant

48 red candy-coated chocolate heart shapes

TO PREPARE THE CUPCAKES Pierce the center of each cake several times with a toothpick and drizzle each with a teaspoon of the liqueur, if using.

TO MAKE THE GANACHE Heat half the cream with the confectioners' sugar in a saucepan until bubbling up around the edges but not boiling. Stir in the chocolate and transfer to a bowl. Let cool, stirring occasionally until the chocolate has melted and the mixture is completely cold. Stir in the remaining cream and chill until thickened.

Before spreading the ganache check its consistency. If it doesn't hold its shape when stirred, beat very lightly with a handheld electric mixer until it just holds its shape. Spread over the cupcakes using a spatula.

TO MAKE THE DECORATION Roll out about a third of the chocolate fondant to ⅛-inch (2.5-mm) thickness on a surface very lightly dusted with confectioners' sugar, keeping the remainder tightly wrapped in plastic wrap. Cut out long strips about ½ inch (1 cm) wide. Cut across into strips that are the diameter of the cake and place a strip over each cake. Position more strips, crossing them over the first.

Reroll the trimmings with half the remaining fondant and cut out more strips. Cut these across into 1¼-inch (3-cm) rectangles, cutting slanting ends on one end of each for ribbon ends. Pinch together the other ends and position two on each cake with the pinched ends meeting in the center to form the bow ends. (Brush the fondant with a dampened paintbrush, if necessary, so they stick.) Roll out the remaining fondant, cut into strips as before, then across into 2-inch (5-cm) lengths. Bend these into loops, pinching the ends together, and position two on each cupcake.

TO FINISH Gently press a heart shape onto the center of each bow to decorate.

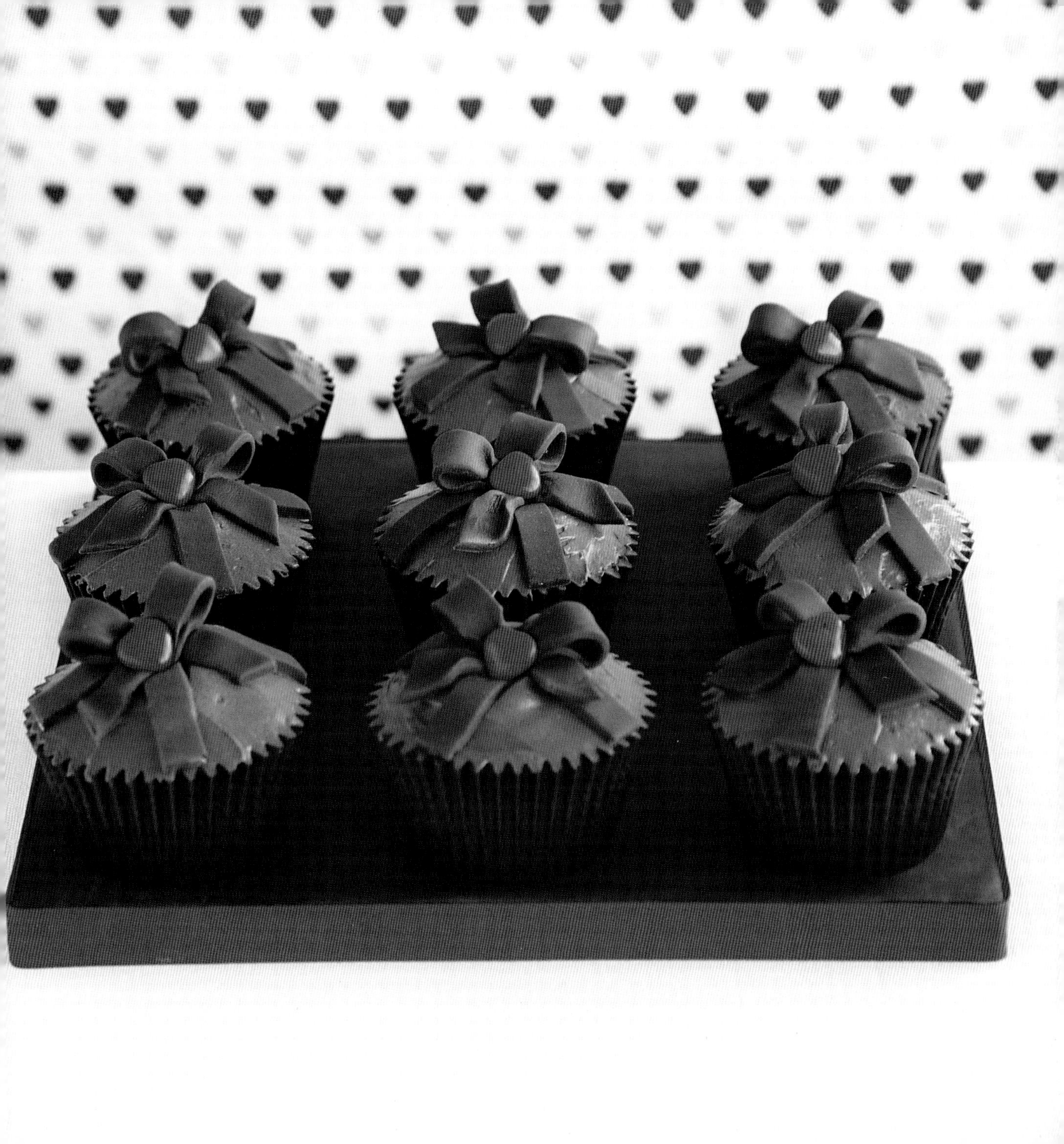

RICH CHOCOLATE SWIRLS

The cups for these wedding cupcakes are pure chocolate, melted and spread over paper baking cups, then peeled away once set. They're are perfect for a small evening wedding party.

SERVES 24
PREPARATION AND DECORATING
TIME about 2½ hours, plus cooling

2¾ lb (1.4 kg) semisweet chocolate, chopped

5 cups (1.2 liters) heavy cream

4 tablespoons confectioners' sugar

6 tablespoons coffee or almond liqueur, or strong coffee

1 quantity (24) Rich Chocolate Cupcakes, see page 5

Chocolate and heart-shaped sugar sprinkles

TO MAKE THE CHOCOLATE CUPS Line two baking sheets with parchment paper. Put 1 lb 10 oz (800 g) of the chocolate in a heatproof bowl. Rest the bowl over a saucepan of gently simmering water, making sure the bowl is not in contact with the water. Heat gently, stirring occasionally until the chocolate has melted. Remove from the heat and let cool for about 10 minutes.

Put about 4 teaspoons of melted chocolate into a paper baking cup and spread the chocolate up the sides until completely coated. Invert the cup onto a paper-lined tray. Repeat with another 23 cups, then make a couple of spares in case of breakages. Chill for about 30 minutes until the chocolate has firmed up, then brush the sides of the cups with the remaining melted chocolate. (If the chocolate has solidified, soften it again over the saucepan of water.) Chill the cups for at least 30 minutes or until completely brittle. Carefully peel away the paper cups and place the chocolate cups on a clean baking sheet.

TO MAKE THE FILLING Whip 1¼ cups (300 ml) of cream with 1 tablespoon of the confectioners' sugar and the liqueur or coffee until just holding its shape. Spoon into the chocolate cups. Peel the paper away from the cupcakes and press a cake gently down into each chocolate cup. (If the cakes are too big for the cups, trim them down slightly so they're only slightly deeper than the chocolate cups.)

TO MAKE THE GANACHE Heat the remaining cream in a saucepan with the remaining confectioners' sugar until bubbling up around the edges but not boiling. Stir in the remaining chocolate and transfer to a bowl. Let cool, stirring occasionally until the chocolate has melted and the mixture is completely cold. Chill until thickened.

TO FINISH Before spreading the ganache check its consistency. If it doesn't hold its shape when stirred, beat very lightly with a handheld electric mixer until it just holds its shape. Put in a large nylon or plastic pastry bag fitted with a large star tip and pipe swirls onto the cupcakes so each cake is completely covered with a thick topping of ganache. Scatter with the sprinkles.

BUTTERFLY CAKES

Red and pink butterflies look stunning against the chocolate frosting on this design. Make them a couple of weeks in advance and finish the decoration up to two days before the wedding.

SERVES 36
PREPARATION AND DECORATING
TIME about 2¼ hours, plus setting
COOKING TIME 1½ hours

Red, pink, and brown food coloring
10 oz (300 g) white rolled fondant
Confectioners' sugar, for dusting
Butter, for greasing
½ cup plus 1 tablespoon (50 g)
  unsweetened cocoa powder
¾ cup plus 2 tablespoons (200 ml)
  boiling water
4 oz (125 g) semisweet chocolate,
  chopped
7 tablespoons (100 g) lightly salted
  butter, softened
1 cup plus 2 tablespoons (250 g)
  firmly packed light brown sugar
2 eggs
1⅓ cups (175 g) self-rising flour
1 quantity Chocolate Buttercream,
  see page 30
1 lb 2 oz (500 g) chocolate-flavored
  rolled fondant
½ quantity Royal Icing, see page 18
1 quantity (24) Rich Chocolate
  Cupcakes, see page 5, baked in
  brown, pink, and red baking cups

TO MAKE THE BUTTERFLIES Line two baking sheets with parchment paper. Knead red food coloring into half the rolled fondant and pink into the other, working on a surface dusted with confectioners' sugar. (Keep both tightly wrapped in plastic wrap until ready to use.)

Roll out the red fondant to ⅛-inch (2.5-mm) thickness on a surface lightly dusted with confectioners' sugar. Cut out butterfly shapes in two sizes, using 2½-inch (6-cm) and 1¼-inch (3-cm) butterfly cutters (measured across wingspan). Transfer to the paper and cut the butterflies in half. Reroll the trimmings to make extras, then make the pink butterflies in the same way. Let harden overnight.

TO MAKE THE LARGE CAKE Grease and line a 6-inch (15-cm) round cake pan, at least 3 inches (7 cm) deep, and preheat the oven to 325°F (160°C). Put the cocoa powder into a bowl and beat in the boiling water. Stir in the chopped chocolate and stir frequently until melted. Beat together the butter and sugar to soften, add the eggs and flour, and beat well to mix. Stir in the chocolate mixture and turn into the pan. Bake for about 1½ hours until a toothpick inserted into the center comes out clean. Let stand in the pan to cool.

Cut the cake in half horizontally and sandwich with a little buttercream. Place the cake on a 6-inch (15-cm) cake card and spread the top and sides with more buttercream. Roll out the chocolate fondant to a 12-inch (30-cm) round. Lift the fondant over the cake and ease around the sides to fit. Smooth the fondant out flat and trim off the excess around the bottom with a knife.

TO FINISH Beat brown food coloring into the royal icing and put in a paper pastry bag. Snip off the tiniest tip. Pipe a ¾-inch (2-cm) line of icing onto the large cake where you want to position a butterfly, and push the two cut edges of a butterfly gently into the piped line to hold it in place. Arrange more butterflies on the large cake. Prop up the wings, if necessary, with toothpicks to secure them until set.

Spread the remaining buttercream over the cupcakes. Arrange butterflies on some of the cupcakes, pushing them gently into the buttercream. Pipe lines of icing along the centers of the butterflies. Arrange the cakes on a tiered cake stand.

WHITE CHOCOLATE AND FROSTED FRUIT

These country-style cupcakes look beautiful on a tiered cake stand with additional fruit arranged in between them. Make sure the fruit are thoroughly dry before arranging over the ganache or the juices will seep into the chocolate and the confectioners' sugar dusting will dissolve.

SERVES 48
PREPARATION AND DECORATING
TIME about 1½ hours

4 cups (1 liter) heavy cream
2¼ lb (1 kg) white chocolate, chopped
2 quantities (48) White Chocolate Cupcakes, see page 4, baked in white and pink baking cups
3¼ lb (1.5 kg) mixture of small berries, e.g. small strawberries, raspberries, and blueberries
Confectioners' sugar, for dusting

TO MAKE THE GANACHE Heat half the cream in a saucepan until bubbling up around the edges but not boiling. Stir in the chocolate and transfer to a bowl. Let cool, stirring occasionally until the chocolate has melted and the mixture is completely cold. Stir in the remaining cream and chill until thickened.

TO DECORATE THE CUPCAKES Before spreading the ganache check its consistency. If it doesn't hold its shape when stirred, beat very lightly with a handheld electric mixer until it just holds its shape. Put in a large pastry bag fitted with a large star tip and pipe swirls onto the cupcakes so that each cake is completely covered with a thick layer of ganache.

Arrange the fruit on top of the ganache and dust lightly with confectioners' sugar.

MIDSUMMER WEDDING

Accompanied with plenty of strawberries, these simple cupcakes can serve as both wedding cakes and seasonal wedding desserts. Decorate the cakes with the chocolate frosting a day in advance so it has time to set a little, and store in a cool place. Arrange the strawberries and flowers several hours before the wedding.

SERVES 24
PREPARATION AND DECORATION
TIME about 1½ hours, plus setting

14 oz (400 g) white chocolate, chopped
⅔ cup (150 ml) milk
2½ cups (300 g) confectioners' sugar
1 quantity (24) White Chocolate Cupcakes, see page 4, baked in white baking cups
13 yards (12 m) fine pink, green, or white ribbon (optional)
Plenty of small strawberries
Edible flowers, to decorate

TO MAKE THE CHOCOLATE FROSTING Put the chocolate in a heatproof bowl with the milk. Rest the bowl over a saucepan of gently simmering water, making sure the bowl is not in contact with the water. Heat very gently, stirring occasionally until the chocolate has melted. Remove from the heat and beat in the confectioners' sugar until smooth. Let stand until cool enough to hold its shape.

TO DECORATE THE CUPCAKES Place the frosting in a large nylon or plastic pastry bag fitted with a large star tip and pipe the frosting over the cupcakes. Alternatively, swirl the frosting over the cupcakes with a spatula knife. Let stand in a cool place to set.

TO FINISH Cut the ribbon, if using, into 20-inch (50-cm) lengths and tie around the cups. Arrange the strawberries on the cupcakes and decorate with edible flowers.

WEDDING RINGS

Shape the rings a week or so in advance so they've plenty of time to set before you make the cakes. Remember to make two rings for each cake, plus a few spares in case of breakages.

SERVES 48
PREPARATION AND DECORATION
TIME about 2 hours, plus setting

Cream food coloring
10 oz (300 g) white rolled fondant
Confectioners' sugar, for dusting
1¾ lb (800 g) white chocolate, chopped
1¼ cups (300 ml) milk
5⅔ cups (700 g) confectioners' sugar
Pale blue dusting powder
2 quantities (48) Vanilla or White Chocolate Cupcakes, see page 4, baked in pale blue or white baking cups

TO MAKE THE RINGS Line two baking sheets with parchment paper. Knead a little cream food coloring into the rolled fondant to a pale shade of ivory on a surface dusted with confectioners' sugar. Thinly roll out half the fondant on a surface lightly dusted with confectioners' sugar (keeping the remainder tightly wrapped in plastic wrap). Cut out ring shapes using 1-inch (2.5-cm) and ¾-inch (2-cm) cutters, using the smaller cutter to cut out the centers of the rings. Transfer the shapes to the paper while you make the remainder using the reserved fondant. Let stand for at least 24 hours to harden.

TO MAKE THE CHOCOLATE FROSTING Put half the chocolate in a heatproof bowl with half the milk. Rest the bowl over a saucepan of gently simmering water, making sure the bowl is not in contact with the water. Heat very gently, stirring occasionally until the chocolate has melted. Remove from the heat and beat in half the confectioners' sugar until smooth. (This quantity is enough to cover half the cupcakes.)

TO FINISH Use a soft paintbrush or your fingers to coat the rings in a fine layer of dusting powder.

Let the frosting stand until cool enough to hold its shape, then spoon a little onto a cupcake and spread it to the edges. While the frosting is still soft, take two of the rings and rest them on top of the frosting so they support each other. Decorate a few of the cupcakes at a time so the frosting is still soft when you arrange the rings.

Use the remaining chocolate, milk, and confectioners' sugar to make a second batch of frosting. Cover and decorate the remaining cakes in the same way.

DAISY CAKES

To save yourself a lot of time, use a daisy plunger cutter, which is much easier to use than ordinary flower cutters (see page 6). They're available from good cookshops and cake decorating suppliers.

SERVES 48
PREPARATION AND DECORATING
TIME about 1¾ hours, plus setting

10 oz (300 g) white rolled fondant
Confectioners' sugar, for dusting
2½ cups (600 ml) heavy cream
1¼ lb (600 g) white chocolate, chopped
2 quantities (48) White Chocolate Cupcakes, see page 4, baked in white or pale yellow baking cups
½ quantity Royal Icing, see page 18
Yellow food coloring

TO MAKE THE DAISIES Line two baking sheets with parchment paper. Very thinly roll out half the fondant on a surface lightly dusted with confectioners' sugar (keeping the remainder tightly wrapped in plastic wrap). Cut out small daisy shapes using ¾-inch (1.5-cm) and ½-inch (1-cm) daisy cutters. Transfer to a lined sheet. Reroll the trimmings with the remaining fondant to make more flowers. You'll need about 12 flowers for each cake. Let stand for several hours or overnight to harden. (Once hard, they can be stored in an airtight container, layers interleaved with paper towels, for up to two weeks.)

TO MAKE THE GANACHE Heat half the cream in a saucepan until bubbling up around the edges but not boiling. Stir in the chocolate and transfer to a bowl. Let cool, stirring occasionally until the chocolate has melted and the mixture is completely cold. Stir in the remaining cream and chill until thickened.

TO FINISH Before spreading the ganache check its consistency. If it doesn't hold its shape when stirred, beat very lightly with a handheld electric mixer until it just holds its shape. Spread over the cupcakes using a spatula.

Arrange the flowers around the edges of the cupcakes. Beat the royal icing in a bowl with a dash of food coloring to make a pale yellow color. Put in a small paper, nylon, or plastic pastry bag fitted with a writing tip and use to pipe dots into the centers of the daisies.

CONVERSIONS

1 teaspoon = 5 ml
1 tablespoon = 15 ml

For those who cook with gas, the temperature conversions you will require when baking the cakes are:

325°F/160°C/Gas Mark 3
350°F/180°C/Gas Mark 4

GLOSSARY

All-purpose flour = plain flour
Apple pie spice = ground mixed spice
Baking cups = cupcake cases
Confectioners' sugar = icing sugar
Dark brown sugar = dark muscovado sugar
Dragées = sugar balls
Fondant sugar = fondant icing sugar
Heavy cream = double cream
Jelly = jam
Light brown sugar = light muscovado sugar
Parchment paper = baking parchment
Pastry bag = piping bag
Plastic wrap = cling film
Rolled fondant = ready-to-roll icing
Self-rising flour = self-raising flour
Semisweet chocolate = plain chocolate
Superfine sugar = caster sugar
Tip = piping nozzle
Toothpick = cocktail stick
Vanilla bean = vanilla pod